Top Service

My Life in Hospitality

Top Service

My Life in Hospitality

SILVANO GIRALDIN

Text Silvano Giraldin
Copyright © Silvano Giraldin

First print November 2024

CONTENTS

FOREWORD — 7

CHAPTER 1: DREAMING BIG — 11

CHAPTER 2: LONDON CALLING — 29

CHAPTER 3: MR GAVROCHE — 49

CHAPTER 4: CULINARY HEIGHTS — 71

CHAPTER 5: GOOD WORK & REWARDS — 89

CHAPTER 6: THE JOURNEY CONTINUES — 103

EPILOGUE: INVISIBLE HEROES—SILVANO'S GUIDE TO SUPERB SERVICE — 109

ABOUT THE AUTHOR — 121

FOREWORD

It's an absolute honour for me to be asked by Silvano to write a testimonial for his biography! This is his story – and somehow over twenty years ago, our paths crossed and became intertwined.

I first met Silvano when I started at Le Gavroche 24 years ago now, as a 23-year-old Commis. And it's as fresh as if it were yesterday. The hustle and bustle of a busy kitchen in morning prep when all of a sudden I hear a thunderous *'Good Morning Everybody!'* It was like a command that had to be answered with a unanimous chorus of *Good Morning Mr Silvano!* It was my first day, in a 2 Michelin Star Kitchen, already overwhelmed by the amount of ingredients arriving from boxes of fish and shellfish, mushrooms, many different animal carcasses and chefs buzzing to and fro.

Silvano always arrived dressed impeccably, with his perfectly combed back net of white hair, he reminded me of an old school Italian character you saw in the GodFather or one of Al Pacino's movies.

It was no secret (which I quickly learnt) that everyone respected Silvano, and also very clear you do not want to upset him.

Silvano's eye for detail would not miss a beat! From the wine glasses to the dressing of a dish that was sent out, when food wasn't coming out fast enough, or in some instances sending food back to the kitchen because it was being sent out too fast! Never mind the poor waiter who forgot to shave that morning or had not ironed a shirt properly.

It was in 2005 when my husband David and I were sent to Mauritius to open Le Gavroche des Tropiques, it was there we really got to know Silvano and his beautiful wife Irene properly.

They came on holiday, and so we spent quite some time together. It was a friendship that has become like family for us. We've watched their two boys grow, get married and have children, and they've known our daughter Anais since birth and as I'm writing this she is about to turn eighteen.

David is a trained sommelier and had also worked many years with Silvano. So conversations about wines, food, restaurants, the hospitality industry were never short. We even travelled away together to some wonderful food and wine destinations.

To this day we still love hearing about the experiences Silvano has had in his time since arriving in London, and I'm so happy that it's been written for others now. As I read his biography, I hear his voice and it's just like he is telling us in person over one of our very long lunches that sometimes have turned to a dinner or going out to another restaurant.

We came to know Silvano as the most amazing Restaurant Manager of the old class that I don't think you see anymore. Ever the perfectionist in delivering excellence in service, with discretion and respect, and a cheeky sense of humour to match.

We have come to love Silvano and Irene as one of our dearest families. Through great times together to the tough times. From advice over the years in our careers to supporting us wherever or in whatever we decided to do.

May those that read this wonderful testament to a true love and life in the service industry find inspiration and wisdom written within these pages.

We love you always, Silvano.

Monica, Anais, David x.

CHAPTER 1: DREAMING BIG

My early years were spent in Casalserugo, a quiet village on the rural outskirts of Padua just a stone's throw away from Venice. Born in 1948, I came into a world that was still emerging from the shadows of war.

My father, Giovanni, had been captured in Greece and then held prisoner near Frankfurt from October 1943 until the end of the war. He never talked about his experiences but I do know he was lucky to survive and that when he arrived home he was virtually a skeleton. He had spent the final three or four months without any food and only survived because my mum, Stefania, had managed to send him parcels of dry bread.

Our family was humble but happy. Along with my two older brothers, Enzo and Ugo, and younger sister Silvana, I helped my parents farm their small piece of land and though we weren't wealthy, the land provided enough fresh produce for us to live well. Pork, chicken and eggs were plentiful thanks to the pigs and chickens we kept. On Fridays, we'd get a welcome change thanks to the fishermen from the nearby port of Chioggia who would arrive laden with the day's catch, which we'd exchange for our own produce or whatever little money we had. It was a simple life but comforting in its familiarity.

My journey into hospitality was launched by a presentation at my school given by the principal of the catering college at Abano Terme, a nearby spa. Aged 14, my school years were ending but I had no idea what I might do next. One of my brothers had become a builder while the other was a masseur, as our parents' farm was too small for farming to be an option for us. Like many of my peers, I might well have taken up a trade such as ironmongery or plumbing. Hospitality was not in my blood, nor were grand ambitions stirring in me, but the idea of catering college caught my attention. The fact that Abano Terme was well-known for its luxury and excellence, plus the principal's talk of opportunity and travel, helped make up my mind. Also, I figured I could immediately start to make money with evening and weekend work within the tourism industry. I signed up.

My enrolment marked the start of a three-year programme that taught the foundation skills of cooking, management and service. Every day I cycled 15 km to and from college, in all weathers, and on evenings and weekends took on waiting work to support myself and contribute towards the household. I soaked up all I was taught but soon realised my passion lay in front of house, rather than the confines of the kitchen or in an office. It wasn't that I disliked cooking, though I wasn't particularly good at it. I just preferred the hustle and bustle of serving guests, meeting new people, creating memorable experiences and the satisfaction of seeing a happy customer. So, I made a conscious decision to focus on the art of service.

The other huge factor in that decision was the influence of two tutors who I came to see as mentors, Mario Trevini and Igino Generali. My admiration for these men, my regard for what they had achieved, what they taught me and the way they presented and conducted themselves, was absolutely instrumental in shaping my aspirations.

Signor Trevini, who spoke five languages and was always impeccably dressed, was married to a Brazilian lady and for six years had served as the personal butler to Juan Peron of Argentina. He had also worked at luxury hotels all over the world and would tell us fabulous tales of his travels and career that made me start to imagine the wider world. Trevini had come to teach at our college in semi-retirement at the age of 60 simply because he wanted to inspire others—which he certainly achieved with me.

Similarly, Signor Generali was winding down from a very successful career working on luxury cruise liners and at top hotels such as The Savoy in London. He too saw teaching as his way of giving back to the industry, and his passion was infectious. His expertise was in mixology and wine, and I have him to thank for sparking my own love and interest in this area. In fact, his teaching educated me to advise my father to plant the Chardonnay vines that are still blessing my family with fantastic wine more than 60 years later.

His wise words also kept me on the straight and narrow for many years after the last time I saw him. He impressed on his students the dangers of alcohol and told us how often you see people in our industry become reliant on it. Thanks to his advice I have always enjoyed drinking and living very well but made sure I knew my limit. Sadly, even after just a short time in the industry, I came to know many others who weren't so lucky.

Trevini and Generali made an enormous impression on me at a vital time in my life and I've remained grateful for their teachings. They told me to always strive for excellence while never losing sight of the joy of serving others. Their belief in me propelled me forward in my own career and, in later years, guided me to work towards inspiring and helping others to join the hospitality industry themselves. In a more practical sense they made me see that, if I was to reach the heights they had, I needed to look ahead. 'Don't look at the money now. Choose your progression carefully and the money will come to you,' they told me. If not for them I may well have set my sights differently: it would have been much easier for me to go and work in a cafe in Piazza San Marco, and I would probably have made more money and tips initially—but there I would have stayed, and I would never have travelled the world. Trevini and Generali inspired me to dream bigger.

At the end of my first year, I took an internship in the Grand Hotel des Bains, a luxury hotel on the Lido of Venice which was the inspiration for the novella *Death in Venice* and where Visconti's film was shot. Trevini was working in the nearby Excelsior Hotel and we kept in touch. When my stint came to an unexpectedly early end in mid-August he got me a job at the Venice Film Festival, which was just about to start.

This was no fancy position: I was selling cigarettes, but it was the best few weeks of my life thus far. I loved the buzz and the atmosphere. The excitement of the festival crowds was intoxicating, and it was wonderful to feel even a small part of something so important and glamorous. Even more, I loved spotting the beautiful, the rich, the famous, and the all-three as they mingled in the streets with the rest of us.

The icing on the cake for me was the day I looked up from my tray to see Frank Sinatra standing before me. He flashed his Hollywood grin as he requested a pack of Marlboro and, trembling just a little, I handed them over. He tucked it in his pocket, then passed me a 10,000 lire note. 'Keep the change,' he grinned and sauntered off. I watched after him, open-mouthed. Half a minute later I was still bathing in the memory and thinking about how I'd tell my family about my brush with stardom when who should come up to me but Dean Martin! I'd like to say I was less nervous this time but that would be a lie. I managed to pass him his cigarettes and then he too passed me a 10,000 lire note—and he too told me to keep the change! Combined, these tips were so enormous that I hid the money from my dad when I got home because I was worried he'd think I'd stolen it. For me, this was one of the best things to have happened in my life so far. I felt blessed to be in proximity of such fame and success, and to meet some of these people was just amazing. What's more, it sparked the desire to delve deeper into the world of top-end hospitality.

After graduating at the top of the class in the spring of 1966, I set off to do just that. My goal at that time was to travel around Europe, learn English, French and German, and eventually return to Venice to work at one of the area's many high-end hotels.

TOP SERVICE

My first paid job after graduating was in Nice at the Hotel Negresco, one of the top hotels in France, where I was no stranger; I had spent the previous summer there, on an internship at the end of my second year at college, and it had been a fantastic learning experience. Very little arrived plated at the Negresco's tables. In the long-held French tradition, much of the food was prepared for serving by the waiter in front of the customer. If somebody asked for a portion of pheasant the whole bird would be brought to the table and carved and deboned there. If someone ordered skate, a whole wing would arrive then prepared for eating. Waiters were expected to peel and segment oranges, cook steak au poivre and prepare crêpes flambé. It was a skilled performance. I learned so much at the Negresco … only by watching though. I wasn't actually allowed to do any of it myself of course. I was too young, too junior to be trusted with such important tasks. But by watching the others I absorbed so much that I then took with me and that I still remember today. At the end of my internship in 1965 the hotel manager said that he liked my attitude and offered me a paid job once I'd finished college, which I happily accepted.

And so, in the summer of 1966, I started work as a proper commis waiter. This was the Swinging Sixties of course, and not long after I arrived at the Hotel Negresco, The Beatles arrived there too. They were in the city for a gig and rented an entire wing of the hotel for themselves and their entourage. I was as starstruck as I had been back at the Venice Film Festival and, though I only really watched from afar, enjoying the occasional glimpse of John, Paul, Ringo or George (I sometimes couldn't tell which) moving around in their suite, it was further confirmation that I was going to love this life.

The next four years were transformative. I crisscrossed France and
Belgium from the Hotel Atlanta in Brussels to the Hotel D'Albion in Aix-les-Bains, the Hotel Le Dahu in Courchevel, and the Hotel Christina in La Plagne. Alternating between the winter ski resorts and the summer warmth, I would return to Padua to reconnect with my family in between seasons. It was always lovely to see them, and their support and encouragement gave me the strength to keep pushing on.

My journey began as *commis de rang* at Hotel Atlanta, a place that, although not the best in its class, taught me valuable lessons about resilience and adaptability. The first weeks were a struggle. Wages and tips were only given out at the end of the month so I was surviving on not much more than thin air, but I made it to payday, my belt a little tighter.

From then on my work followed a pattern. Summers were spent in the picturesque town of Aix-les-Bains at Hotel D'Albion, a spa town in the Savoy region where I did well, rising through the ranks from *commis de rang*, to *chef de rang*, to *sommelier*. The winters, on the other hand, saw me in the heart of the French Alps, working at Hotel Le Dahu in Courchevel and Hotel Christina in La Plagne. The seasonal nature of my work and its rhythm provided a nice balance, and its variety helped me hone my craft and further my knowledge about wine, an interest that would grow significantly over the years.

There were other challenges in those early days. The distance from family, the temptation to fall in with the wrong crowd, and the rigorous demands of the job occasionally made me question my choices. Hours were long, and I often worked breakfast, lunch and dinner services with minimal breaks in between. Living arrangements varied and could be challenging. Sometimes I was fortunate to have lodging provided by the hotel while at other times, accommodation was basic and shared with lots of others which meant little privacy—but often great camaraderie.

The summer of 1968 saw disruption across France in the form of strikes and student uprisings. Transport was greatly affected, which, in turn, affected tourism, and the summer season at Hotel D'Albion ended early season. I decided to escape the chaos and return home to my family, but of course, there were no trains. So, I hitchhiked all the way to Geneva where trains were running and then travelled back to Padua in relative comfort. Thankfully I was able to return to Aix-les-Bains, and work, after a short time. It was all part of the experience though, and each challenge tested my resilience and my ability to stay professional.

It was easy to be swayed by the after-work nightlife that was an intrinsic part of the hospitality industry then as it is now. I enjoyed many great nights out with workmates but learned to balance my social life with a strong focus on my career. Sadly, along the way, I saw many colleagues succumb to the pitfalls of excessive drinking or other vices: talented people losing their way, unable to maintain the discipline required for success.

Whenever my work ethic wavered I thought of the words of Trevini and Generali, and another valued colleague I met along the way who became a mentor to me, the ex-army *maître d'* at Hotel D'Albion. Each had instilled in me the importance of humility, continuous learning, and striving for excellence. Their advice to always seek out the best opportunities, and forget about the money for now, resonated with me and guided my career decisions. This mindset pushed me to always aim to work in top-tier establishments, continually pushing myself to reach the pinnacle of the industry.

Despite the long hours and demanding schedules, I got a lot of satisfaction from the work, and I quickly moved up from entry-level positions to more responsible roles, learning about wine and refining my skills in table service. The seasonal nature of the job meant that though there were intense periods of long hours and hard physical work, these were followed by substantial breaks, during which I returned to Italy to help my family on the farm. Back home in Padua, I was able to rest, recharge and reconnect with my roots.

In the summer of '69, a *maître d'* friend suggested I work in Paris, and this turned out to be an incredible experience—though it didn't begin well. Initially, I found a reasonable job in a reasonable establishment but struggled to find decent lodgings. I was turning up to work looking unkempt and feeling tired and stressed and, unsurprisingly, I was sacked—the one and only time in my life! It was a harsh lesson but I didn't blame the hotel: I wasn't performing well. The experience taught me a very important lesson that I thought back to many times in my later career when I was looking after staff myself: to excel, front-of-house staff need to be content and well-supported in their personal lives. If they're not happy at home it shows at work, and that's not good for anyone.

I quickly found another position, but this wasn't ideal either. After a few months of struggle, I contacted the *maître d'* friend and he provided me with a better position, with accommodation, at Auberge du Coeur Volant in Louveciennes.

This was a fantastic hotel, popular with tourists thanks to its great location between Château de Marly and the Palace of Versailles, and I stayed for over a year. At last, I got to fully appreciate and enjoy living and working in vibrant Paris.

My time at Auberge du Coeur Volant was particularly formative because it was where I mastered the art of tableside preparations. Since catering school, I had been learning and practising skills that were then vital in waiting, such as preparing Crêpes Suzette, deboning, a chicken and carving a pheasant in front of the guests. In those days if somebody ordered a portion of pheasant the whole bird would be brought to the table and the waiter would debone it there in front of them, asking what they wanted: 'You like the leg?', 'The breast for you Madam?' and so on. I was good at these things but hadn't yet been trusted to do them in front of customers, which was tiresome at The Negresco, as nothing came to the table on a plate ready to eat. I'd had to 'watch and learn' as more senior colleagues did such important things. But at Auberge I was finally seen as experienced enough to perform at the tableside, and it felt fantastic. What's more, in the 14 months I worked there I rose from *chef de rang* to *maître d'*. Now, having worked at this level and as a *sommelier* at Hotel D'Albion, I felt I was really getting somewhere.

Throughout my time working around Europe, I continually honed my craft, developed a deep understanding of the hospitality industry and rose through the ranks—but I knew that to advance further, I needed to speak English. I wrote off to several top hotels in London including The Savoy and Claridge's—but in French!—and unsurprisingly received no responses. It was disheartening.

One day in October 1970 I was talking to a waiter who had just returned from England. He told me I was wasting my time applying to the big established hotels—they had plenty of staff and didn't need to waste time with those like me who couldn't speak the language. He had a better idea: the London restaurant scene was buzzing with talk of two young French brothers, Michel and Albert Roux. They were relatively new to the city but their restaurants already had excellent reputations and they were rapidly expanding their operations. They liked to employ French-speaking staff and needed more: I should try them.

I jumped at the idea and immediately fired off a nice little letter to them—in French. Within a week I received a reply: '*Viens ici et travaille pour nous,*' the letter said. 'Come here and work for us.' They wanted me to start work as *commis de rang* at Le Gavroche in Chelsea, one of the four businesses that the brothers had established in London, as soon as possible.

I didn't need asking twice. They set about arranging a green card for me and as soon as it was cleared I booked my ferry ticket, gave my notice and packed a small bag. I was excited. I was headed for London and had a feeling that great things were coming—and as it turned out, I was right.

My family in 1951

Early year at school

Stage at the Negresco Hotel in Nice

In Courchevel 1968

Brussels 1967

La Plagne 1969

CHAPTER 2: LONDON CALLING

My arrival in London was inauspicious. It was a grey, damp day in January 1971 when I took the train from Paris to Calais and then the ferry to Dover. Going through Customs I discovered that my Green Card didn't automatically grant me entry into the UK: I had to be inspected by a doctor and have my teeth checked over before being waved through.

By the time I stepped out of the taxi at 61 Lower Sloane Street in Chelsea, where Le Gavroche was at that time, I was cold and tired after a journey that had taken the best part of a day. The restaurant didn't look like much from the outside: on the junction of a few roads, it was housed in a double-fronted space on the ground floor of a rather flat, grey 20th-century construction that stood across from a block of much grander, taller red-brick buildings with turrets and bay windows. But I knew enough already to appreciate that what was special about the restaurant I was about to become a part of was not its bricks and mortar.

Le Gavroche had opened four years previously, in 1967, but was already regarded as a beacon of high-quality French cuisine in London. Albert and Michel Roux, aged just 35 and 30, had already established a worldwide reputation. Alongside Le Gavroche, they had two other London restaurants: Les Poulbot in Cheapside which was recognised at the time by Egon Ronay being one of the top places in London to eat; Brasserie Benoit, later known as Le Gamin, near Fleet Street and the Law Courts; and a delicatessen near Le Gavroche called Le Cochon Rose. By the early '70s, Albert and Michel already employed nearly 100 people. The following year they would open the Waterside Inn at Bray.

I made my way into the restaurant. It was midday and though Le Gavroche in those days didn't open for lunch people were busying around, talking in French, easing my initial fears about my poor English. The space was small, seating only about 50, but it was elegant and stylish, with some fine lithographs on the wall and even, I was to discover, a Picasso.

A smartly dressed man approached me, his hand held out to shake mine. '*Ciao!* Silvano?' he queried. I smiled and felt my shoulders relax a little more. He introduced himself as Angelo Poletti, the restaurant's Italian manager, and in the coming days and weeks, he would really help me settle in.

Angelo explained that I would start work at 3 p.m. the next day. The brothers had arranged temporary accommodation for me to stay in while I found something more permanent. I was to wait for the boss who would arrive at some point to take me there. He fetched me a coffee and I tucked myself into a corner to wait. An hour or two passed and I was starting to feel uncomfortable when a short, dark, stocky man in a blood-stained white kitchen coat, with a cigarette hanging from his lips, pushed through the door from the kitchen and approached me. I assumed he was a member of staff. 'Come on, let's go,' he said.

'No,' I replied. 'Thanks, but I'm waiting for the boss.'

The man looked at me with intense eyes. He turned and continued on. 'I am the boss!' he called behind him as he went. 'I've just got back from Smithfield Meat Market. Come on. Follow me!'

I was shocked. I'd been expecting someone older, taller, in a shirt and tie. I grabbed my bag and scuttled after him. Albert Roux and I were to work very closely together for the next nearly 50 years, but of course, I had no idea of that then. All I knew was that our unusual first meeting left a lasting impression on me.

Those first few weeks went by quickly. The accommodation was decent, and it was great living in the heart of London at such a vibrant time. What's more, the Roux brothers, apparently seeing potential in me, supported me in my drive to learn English by paying for me to attend daytime lessons at International House. Thanks to this, my grasp of the language improved very quickly.

At 3 p.m. each afternoon, I would arrive at Le Gavroche ready for the dinner shift—right from the start, I knew that the restaurant was exactly the place that I needed to be. The food, the wine, the standards of service—all were absolutely top-drawer.

But if anything confirmed the high-end status of Le Gavroche for me it was the calibre of the guests. One evening in my first year there I answered the phone to hear the concierge at The Savoy on the other end.

'Look,' he said. 'I have a very important guest who needs a table for two tonight. You've got to take them.'

'We can't,' I said. 'We're fully booked.'

He was having none of it. 'If I told you the name, you'd have to book him in.'

I could hear he meant business. 'Let me ask my manager if we have room,' I said and set off to find Angelo.

When I found him Angelo shrugged his consent. 'Yes,' he said. 'We will always find room if they're important, and The Savoy can be trusted when they tell us they are.'

I trotted back to the phone. 'We have room,' I told the concierge. 'Can I have the name please?'

'Charlie Chaplin,' he replied.

A few hours later this legend of stage and screen arrived, his extremely young wife in tow. They sat quietly at their table and appeared to enjoy their meal—they finished it at least—but didn't say as much to the staff. When they were done they stood to leave and I got the courage to ask. 'Did you enjoy your meal, Mr Chaplin?'

He just looked at me and said, 'Book us in for tomorrow night.' He dined with us five nights in a row that week. On the final night, he asked for the Visitors' Book. 'It's wonderful,' he wrote and dashed off his signature below. A few years later Robert Redford dined with us and asked to see the book, a big, gold tome filled with messages from the great and good. He went through all the pages and stopped at Charlie Chaplin's words, then asked for a pen. 'Me too,' he wrote underneath, then signed it too.

By the time I'd been at Le Gavroche a few months, it felt like I'd seen everyone who was anyone come in through the doors. We had them all: David Bowie, The Rolling Stones (only once, as they refused to conform to the dress code), The Beatles, and their manager, an American guy called Alan Klein, who parked his white Rolls-Royce outside and spent a fortune in wine—easily £1,000 pounds on one bottle, which would be around £20,000 today.

And though the food and wine were fantastic what really drew the rich and famous in was the atmosphere—it was electric. The buzz in that room was like nothing I'd experienced before. The hum of conversation, the heads turning to see who was at the next table and who had just walked in the door, the glint of the low lighting bouncing off diamonds—diners were there to see and be seen as much as to eat.

The atmosphere behind the scenes was no less exciting. The forward-thinking Roux brothers only employed young staff as eager to innovate as they were and as a result things felt new and fresh, fast-paced and we were constantly striving for better. The team was encouraged to be adaptable and forward-thinking, to embrace new techniques and ideas, ensuring that Le Gavroche remained at the forefront of the culinary scene. We all worked very hard.

The brothers had revolutionized dining in the few years they had been in London, in a number of ways. The menu at Le Gavroche was comparatively very small, which was totally innovative—and extremely brave! If you went to the other big-name restaurants of the time, Mirabelle say, or The Savoy Grill, or the Connaught Hotel, there would be 20 starters, 20 to 30 main courses and 30-odd desserts to choose from. Minimum. The Roux Brothers cut this up: they offered 10 starters, 10 mains, 10 desserts—that was it. Streamlined. Also, the restaurant only opened in the evenings; Chelsea was a residential area, and so there simply wasn't the business trade to make lunchtimes viable. But what they did offer was absolutely perfect and of the highest quality. The food was produced to a standard that you simply could not find anywhere else in the UK. In those days, and for many more years to come, the Roux brothers really were the avant-garde of the food industry in this country.

The restaurant became more to me than just a workplace; it was a community, a family, and a place where dreams were realised. And as I settled into my role I realised that Le Gavroche was not just the right place for me—it was a place where I could grow, learn and carve a niche in this seat of culinary excellence. Though I had begun working there as a *commis de rang*, I was quickly promoted to *chef de rang*, to *maître d'*, then—no small thanks to the fact that after my English lessons ended the brothers and Michel in particular helped me develop my wine expertise—to *sommelier*.

In 1974 Michelin published its first guide to Britain since 1931, and Le Gavroche gained its first star for fine dining, thanks to a team that included my good friend Jean Pierre Durantet as restaurant manager led of course by Albert and Michel. The writeup in the guide applauded our restaurant's outstanding food, impeccable service and unique atmosphere, and of course we were absolutely thrilled to be in there—though also a little puzzled to be ranked alongside two dozen other restaurants that, though good, were undeniably not of the same exceptional standard.

That was corrected in 1977 when we received our second star, alongside only one other, The Connaught, which were very happy to be compared to. This recognition was a testament to the hard work and dedication of the entire team and solidified Le Gavroche's position as one of the top restaurants in the country. I believe that in part this second star also came about because by now we had a world-class sommelier on the team in the form of John Jackson, and my excellent assistant manager Jean Claude Peschaud, who was tough but fair and very good at ensuring that our standards never wavered. Though Gavroche had always had an excellent front-of-house team now it felt like we had the Dream Team.

Before the second star, in 1975, I had been made restaurant manager, with my role involving more than just overseeing the day-to-day operations. To me, the ambience of the restaurant is as important as the quality of the food. I worked to create a magical atmosphere where every customer, no matter who they were, felt important, from the moment they arrived. Each guest was welcomed with open arms and as I was very good at recognising faces (and had tricks up my sleeve for the odd occasion when someone's name escaped me) I could often greet people by name, which they loved. They would grow in stature in front of their guests, they'd be smiling, we'd get them their first drink and they'd relax. They'd look around the room, humming with conversation punctuated with low laughter, and see royalty on one table, a Hollywood film star on another, a rich sheikh and his wives on another, and know they were in the very best restaurant in the country. Yet they also felt at home.

That's not to say that the food was unimportant, of course not; a restaurant will not survive without good food. You need to have top chefs, and that's what we had with Albert and Michel and the many marvellous chefs he had working under him over the years. In the Chelsea restaurant, we had Denis Lobry, Christian Delteil, Jean Louis Paul, Pierre Koffmann, Marc Beaujeu, Jean Louis Taillebaud, Marco Pierre White. But the atmosphere of the restaurant is also incredibly important and a lot of a lot of chefs forget about that. I was the conductor, making sure that the alchemy of the kitchen was presented as magical for the guests. Of course, there were many talented front-of-house staff working to create the magic too, including, over the years, David Ridgeway, Diego Masciaga, Jean Claude Breton, Remy Lyse and Michel Lang.

The presence of royalty, celebrities, politicians, business leaders and the super-rich created a buzz around Le Gavroche, but it was the dedication to quality and innovation that kept them coming back. The restaurant became a symbol of excellence in the culinary world, setting standards that others aspired to meet, and was a melting pot of cultures and ideas. The Roux brothers, with their French roots, brought a distinct culinary style to London, which was embraced and celebrated by a diverse clientele.

By the end of the '70s, Gavroche was firmly ensconced in its position at the centre of London's high-end social scene and many remarkable people passed through its doors. One night we had a particularly stellar crowd in. *My Fair Lady* had recently opened at the Adelphi Theatre and to celebrate, British peer and banker Lord Rothschild, who was a regular diner, was hosting a table of 10 guests that included the English actor Rex Harrison—who had starred in the original production—and Soviet-born dancer Rudolph Nureyev, known as ballet's 'Enfant Terrible.' They were having a very lively time and there was much chatter and laughter. However, there was one guest, a very beautiful girl, who seemed to be irritating some of the people around the table. She was being very loud, disrupting the conversation, giggling incessantly and sitting on laps—she seemed to be determined to go home with one of the men in the group though didn't seem to care which.

After a time I saw one of the group lean over to Nureyev and whisper in his ear. The dancer nodded and stood up abruptly. There was a screech as his chair fell back but he took no notice, marched round the table, grabbed the girl's arm, hauled her off someone's lap and dragged her to the front door of the restaurant. He wrenched it open and threw her out to the street where she lay sprawled, her handbag at her feet. Someone handed Rudolph the girl's coat and he threw it out after her.

'That's where you belong, dahling!' he called then slammed the door and stalked back to the table, where he was met with a round of applause, and not just from his own table.

There is a postscript to this story. More than 20 years later I was reading an article in the *New York Times* about the recently-published memoirs of an American journalist. The journalist loved to eat well and had eaten at Le Gavroche on a number of occasions, and he was asked about his most memorable meal—and he recounted the above story, as he too had been in Gavroche that night!

From the very early days of my time there I had become used to serving and then welcoming peers, members of the aristocracy and even royalty—and there certainly were some very memorable incidents. One evening in my first year Peter Sellers, who I also came to know as a regular, arrived at the restaurant and was seated at his usual table, number 11 in the corner. That night Michel was at front of house and Albert was in the kitchen as at that time the brothers were alternating roles.

Just a few minutes later an attractive, dark-haired, well-dressed lady in her early 40s swept through the door. Her nose in the air, she took no notice whatsoever of Michel and marched haughtily by, headed for Mr Sellers at table 11. Michel wasn't sure what to do. He hesitated, not used to being ignored. He turned to the *maître d'* and opened his mouth to voice his displeasure only for Jean-Pierre to shut him down. 'Be quiet,' he hissed. 'It's Princess Margaret!'

Table 11 was definitely the best in the house, and the most frequently requested, but of course not everyone could have it. Many people had their favourite table but it was accepted that if you were a 'normal' person you might get bumped off it if someone high-profile got to it first. One time it had been booked by a man called Andrew Grima who was a jeweller to Queen Elizabeth, a very regular customer. He was a very nice man and would come in with a different beautiful woman on his arm every time. On this particular occasion, he had booked table 11 but when he arrived, he was told it was no longer available.

He looked a little irritated, obviously embarrassed in front of his pretty young date. 'But that's the table I booked,' he said (but not too vehemently, as he was regular enough to know that this was how things were sometimes at Le Gavroche).

'Sorry Mr Grima,' I said apologetically. 'I cannot give you that table.'

'Okay, I understand,' he said and smiled. 'They'd better be important for you to have given them my table.'

'Well,' I said. 'If you take a look when you go in I'm sure you'll understand.'

Again, it was Peter Sellers dining with the princess. Far from being offended, Mr Grima was impressed: it was a sign of his good taste that people of that calibre liked to dine where he did. He actually went over to the pair to say hello because at some time he had made something for Princess Margaret—and he got to introduce his young lady to them too. He still went away a happy man that night.

Working at Le Gavroche was not without its challenges. The restaurant industry is known for its high-pressure and demanding environment, and I faced numerous obstacles, from problems with staff and upset customers to dealing with unexpected events … like the night an IRA kidnap victim turned up in our kitchen.

It was the mid-'70s, just a year or so after Walton's Restaurant had been destroyed by a bomb that killed two people and injured 23 others. As a result of that incident many other Chelsea businesses had protective grills installed in their windows that looked like chicken wire—not a good look but a necessary measure, I suppose.

One evening I was on the restaurant floor when a waiter approached me and hissed that I had to go into the kitchen. Nothing prepared me for what I saw. The kitchen was in uproar and in the middle of it all stood a bedraggled man bound at the wrists, knees and ankles, blindfolded and with a gag in his mouth. The hunt was on for a pair of scissors to set him free.

For a second I thought it was a joke, until someone explained what had happened. Apparently the washer-up, a very nice Algerian guy called Saïd (who went on to become a barman at the Savoy) had heard knocking on the door that led out to the yard, opened it, and found the guy tapping on it with his head. Once he was freed we found out that he was a British soldier from the nearby Chelsea Barracks who had been captured by the IRA and held captive but then for some reason he had been 'freed' by being dumped in one of our bins; luckily he'd managed to escape from it before someone could dump 10 pounds of fish guts on his head.

We released his bindings and fed him, then found him a phone so he could call the police ... and they sprung into action. There was great concern that there would be another explosion, so our restaurant and the buildings on either side were evacuated, meaning that guests had to leave their meals half-eaten. Most went on home and some came with the staff to the Rose and Crown pub across the road to wait until we were allowed back in. The police took so long to satisfy themselves that all was well that by the time we got the all-clear there was just one customer remaining with us in the pub: an American guy who had been in a number of times before named Colonel Demuth, an ex-CIA and who had been a colonel during the Second World War. He was the only person who waited out the whole time, just so he could come back for his pudding which he had already ordered: the tarte tatin. I think that says a lot about how good the tarte tatin was at Le Gavroche.

Though I'm dropping a few names in here, being discrete was an important part of working at the restaurant. It was important that guests knew that what happened in the dining room (or toilets!) of Le Gavroche, what was said there and who they were with would not leave those four walls. However, many, many years have passed since those days and sadly, many of the people from those days are no longer with us. And many of my stories from those days don't put anyone in a bad light—quite the contrary. But for those that do I have a saying: you can tell the sin just not the sinner. Such as the time when a very important person arrived with his mistress expecting to sit at his favourite spot only to be told that he couldn't have it. He was a little indignant. 'Why am I not being given my usual table?' he asked.

I walked him away from his girlfriend to a discreet corner where he could see his usual table without being seen. 'Look over there,' I said. There was his wife, dining at his favourite table with her toyboy. Two or three months later I saw in the paper that the couple had separated.

Someone else who came in regularly with his mistress was a successful printer. One evening his son arrived and, thinking it was a nice thing to do, I gave the son his dad's regular table. Half an hour later the dad turned up at the door with his mistress and asked for his usual table.

'No,' I said. 'In fact, I'm not even going to let you into the restaurant.'

'Why on earth not?' he asked.

I took him by the elbow and steered him away so I could talk to him discretely. 'Your son is downstairs having dinner with his wife. Do you want to have a family problem?' He took his mistress and ran away very quickly.

Alongside promotions and taking on extra responsibility at work, by the late '70s, my home life had drastically moved on. After my first few weeks in the accommodation provided for me, I found decent lodgings in a nice Victorian house just a 15-minute walk from the restaurant at 113 St George's Square in Pimlico. OK, it was expensive compared to some places at the time but nothing like now. Even on a waiter's wages it was affordable—and I was living around the King's Road, the absolute beating heart of London at what was a very exciting time in the city. It was fantastic and, though we worked extremely hard at the restaurant, we did also manage some great nights out.

In 1973 I met Irene and in 1979 we married. Albert insisted on throwing us a lunchtime reception at Le Gavroche and then a cocktail party in the evening. Irene had also worked in the industry—at Le Poulbot, amongst other places—so understood the life and the pressures, but she put her career on hold so we could raise a family. Our first son Alexander was born in 1980 followed by Sebastian in 1983.

There is no way that I could have had any sort of family life had it not been for Irene and her unending support. She was the force behind me, she raised our sons virtually without me at times and gave me the peace of mind to know that all was taken care of at home so that I could concentrate on work. In comparison with what Irene had to do, my role at work was very easy. I was only able to give my very best because, thanks to Irene, I had a very happy and settled home life. I consider myself incredibly lucky. My parents gave me support to focus on work when I was a young man and then my wife did it once more once I was an adult.

By the start of the new decade I, and Le Gavroche, had come a long way. But there was much more yet to come.

Sommelier at Gavroche 1973

Tradition & Quality reception at Gavroche 1976

Le Gavroche 1976 with John Jackson, Jacky Cognet, Alain Lacouture

Special event with Bertrand Barra, Mazzone Trifone

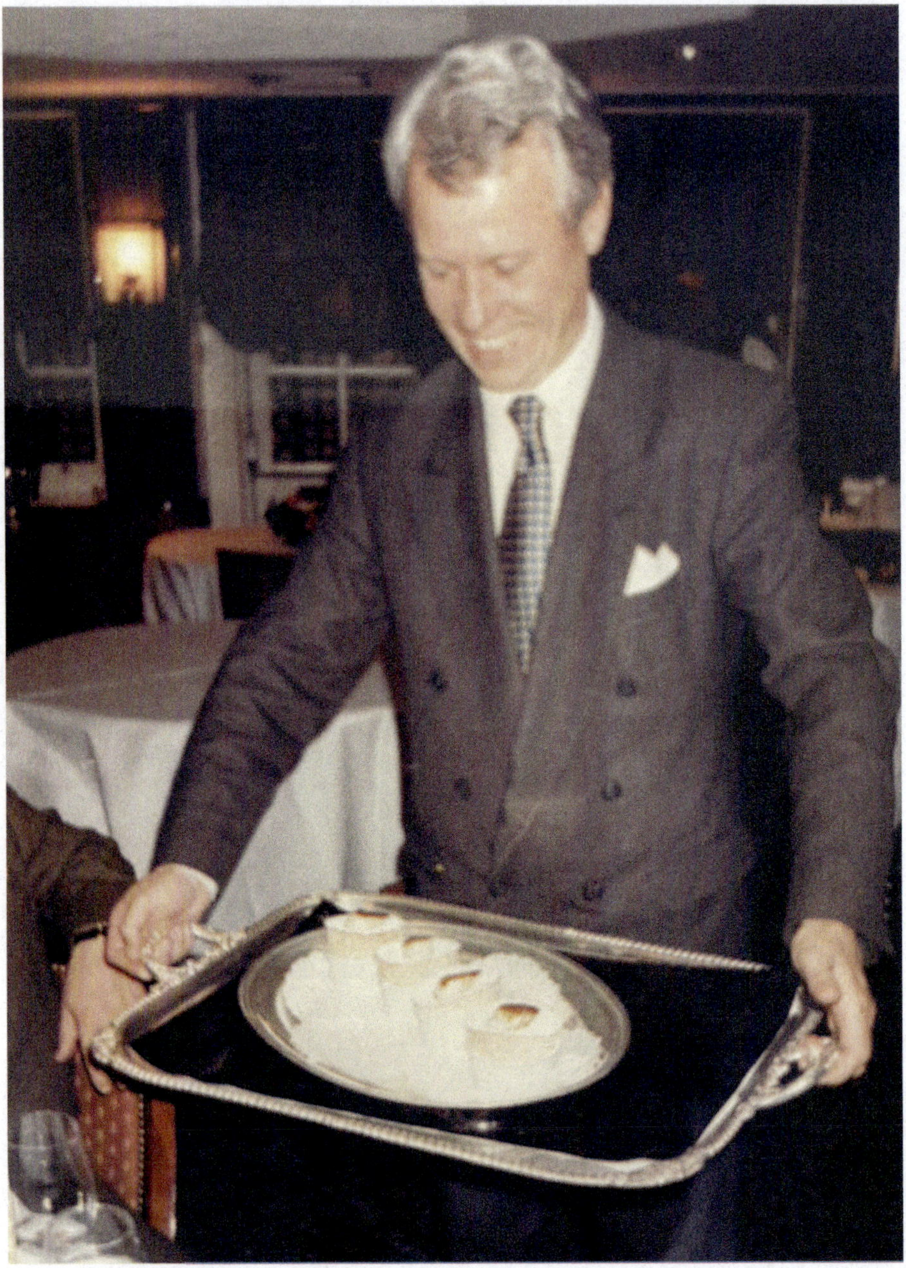

CHAPTER 3: MR GAVROCHE

In the spring of 1981, Le Gavroche embarked on a significant change that would further elevate its status in the culinary world. The decision to move from its original location in Chelsea to a larger, more opulent setting at 43 Upper Brook St in Mayfair was driven by both necessity and ambition. The landlord's decision to raise the rent forced Albert and Michel to find new premises, but it also gave us the opportunity to expand and enhance the restaurant's offerings. The new location, again a corner setting but now in a bustling business district and close to Hyde Park, would allow Le Gavroche to serve both lunch and dinner in a more luxurious atmosphere.

The transition was seamless. We closed the Chelsea location on a Saturday night and, thanks to meticulous planning and a dedicated team, opened the new Mayfair premises the following Monday. From then on we were busier than we had ever been. The move enabled us to elevate the entire experience and everyone wanted to come and see the new place.

The Mayfair restaurant was designed by the same interior decorator as Chelsea, David Mlinaric, who had previously worked on projects for the National Trust, and retained the charm and elegance of the original, the continuity ensuring that our loyal patrons felt at home in the new environment.

Again there was banquette seating with semi-circular tables and a few round tables for four in the middle with all the twos or threes around the edges. As in Chelsea, we had bottle green and burgundy decor and colonial bamboo trim, and the artwork also echoed the old establishment with Picasso, Miró and Dalí. The lighting, the fixtures, the seating arrangements —all contributed to an unforgettable dining experience. The restaurant's layout now seated more people but its L-shaped design created intimacy, so there was a lively atmosphere. It was a place where conversations flowed, deals were made, and memories were created. Customers loved the 'new' Gavroche and its reputation as the place to see and be seen only grew.

The addition of lunch service proved to be immensely popular. Now in a more vibrant part of the city, we became the go-to spot for business lunches and evening dinners. Initially, to balance this, we closed on weekends, allowing the staff to enjoy a well-deserved break and time with their loved ones. This decision was later reconsidered, but those early years set a precedent for work-life balance in the hospitality industry.

Le Gavroche continued to innovate and adapt to changing trends and tastes. In the early 1980s, we were among the first to plate dishes in the kitchen rather than at the table, allowing for more creativity in presentation, better portion control and more streamlined service. This shift was part of our commitment to staying ahead of the curve and providing our guests with the best possible dining experience.

TOP SERVICE

In May 1982, the hard work paid off spectacularly when Le Gavroche was awarded its third Michelin star, making it the first restaurant in Britain to receive such an honour. This was a momentous achievement and solidified our place at the pinnacle of the culinary world. The recognition was a testament to the exceptional skills of our chefs, particularly René Bajard and Steven Docherty, whose ability to execute Albert's vision flawlessly ensured the highest standards were maintained even in Albert's absence. But it wasn't only about the food; it was about the entire dining experience, from the moment guests walked through our doors to the time they left.

This period is now remembered as a critical time for the UK food scene—and we were leading the way. We had no trouble attracting talented and ambitious people to our team. Over the years we would see many great chefs working in the Mayfair restaurant, some of whom became household names, including Rowley Leigh, Steven Doherty, Gordon Ramsay, Marcus Wareing, Marc Prescot, Brian Maule, Bryn William, Nicolas Laridan, Monica Galetti and Rachel Humphrey. All count Gavroche as an important step in their illustrious careers and credit it with helping them hone their skills. It was a privilege to mentor these young talents, guiding them as they embarked on their culinary journeys.

The 1980s is also notorious for its thriving economy, glamour, successes and excesses. It was a wonderful time for many members of the elite, for the rich, famous and powerful—and I was welcoming them all through the doors. In his own memoir Fred Sirieix, a top-class front-of-house professional who worked at a few Roux establishments including on my team at Le Gavroche and who is now best known for his TV appearances, referred to me as 'Mr Gavroche,' a name that fills me with pride. I was the face of Le Gavroche, the ambassador between the kitchen and our guests. My role was to ensure that every diner felt welcomed and cherished, a task I took immense pride in.

Of course, I had a great team working tirelessly alongside me at the Mayfair restaurant too, and many of these went on to achieve great things elsewhere, such as Diego Masciaga, Jean Claude Breton, Vincent Rouard, Thierry Georgeau, Emmanuel Perignon, Fred Sirieix, Peter Davis, Michael Newton Young, Thierry Tomasin, Emmanuel Landre, Francois Bertrand and David Galetti.

Jean Claude Peschaud was still alongside me as my right-hand man, ensuring that our standards never wavered. When I was away he kept Le Gavroche running as well as when I was there. He had eyes everywhere and could be very tough with the staff. I remember once that when Fred Sirieix worked with us he came to me to complain that Jean Claude had kicked him! 'I don't even know why!' he said. 'He just came up to me and cracked me in the shin!' He was quite upset.

I calmed him down and then said, 'Look, I'm sorry but that's Jean Claude. He's not perfect but ... he has a lot of qualities. Just learn from him.' Fred soon got over it. Jean Claude was Jean Claude, and I was very fond of him.

Le Gavroche became an institution, a place where history was made and memories were created. We never saw empty seats, except for the night of Charles and Diana's wedding when Park Lane was blocked off and we had to close. It wasn't all bad though—to celebrate, there was a wonderful firework display in Hyde Park, and the staff all went to watch that instead!

Princess Diana was a regular guest, slipping in and out through the back door to avoid the paparazzi. She began coming in just after she married Charles with her good friend Sir Richard Attenborough who was teaching her how to behave in the highest echelons of society. They would come in every couple of weeks and we got to know her quite well—she was very warm and friendly.

One evening she arrived for dinner and, as I was showing her down the steps to the dining room, she spotted a new hanging on the wall: a framed certificate documenting an honourary doctorate that Albert had been awarded by the University of Bournemouth

Diana stopped briefly and leaned in to read what the certificate said then turned to me, her eyes twinkling. 'A doctorate for Albert?' she smiled, mischievously, 'What is he, a doctor of spaghetti?' She did like to tease people.

At Le Gavroche, we were not strangers to royalty. Queen Elizabeth II dined at the restaurant once, though I wasn't there that day, and Queen Elizabeth, The Queen Mother, dined with us very regularly from the early days in Chelsea and continued to do so in Mayfair as we were now closer to Clarence House, her London home.

She always sat at the same table, number 14 in the middle of the room so she could overlook the entire restaurant, and ate the same thing: our signature dish, Soufflé

Suissesse. Albert had been making this dish, a twice-baked cheese soufflé with a rich creamy sauce, since he worked for the Cazalet family, who trained the Queen Mother's horses. It was our most popular dish and never left the menu: however, she refused to call it by that name. When I asked her what she would like she would always reply: 'Tell the chef I want "My Souffle."' It always made me smile.

Barbara Cartland came in often—but the way she dressed, always fully made up with her hair perfectly coiffured, dressed in pastel colours and adorned with pearls, meant that other customers, particularly Americans, would mistake her for royalty. 'Who's that,' they'd ask, all excited. 'Is it the queen?'

Celebrities continued to flock to our restaurant too. If someone was the talk of the town you could be sure their name would be on the booking list. We were so used to seeing the rich and famous dotted around the room that to an extent the extraordinary became routine … though there was one moment which left my feathers a little ruffled.

It was late one morning and we were just about to open for lunch. In one corner of the dining room, I was just finishing briefing my staff with a reminder of who were were expecting on that day. 'Roger Moore will be joining us,' I said. Seeing one young Italian lad looking a little blank I tried to jog his memory. 'You know, 007.' He still looked one the wiser. I raised my eyebrows. 'Bond,' I said, in a low voice that I hoped sounded a little like the suave secret agent from the popular films.

'The name's James Bond.' For a split second, I thought I must have performed a great impression, as the little semicircle of staff looked more amused than I expected—until I felt a tap on my shoulder. I spun round to see Roger Moore himself, a wry smile on his face and one eyebrow raised.

'Here I am,' he said, doing a much better impression of himself than I had managed.

He thought it very funny—as did the staff—but if there had been a hole in the ground I would have gladly climbed into it. Moments like these were the essence of Le Gavroche.

Business was thriving for Britain—and us too. When Le Gavroche had decamped from Lower Sloane Street to Upper Brook Street the lease had not expired so, rather than leave the building empty, the brothers opened 'Gavvers' (the 'Sloane Rangers' affectionate nickname for Le Gavroche) in the old location, with Albert's son Michel Jnr as head chef. This was intended to be a more accessible version of the original restaurant, still with great French food but offered as a set menu at a lower price. It was a great success.

There was more. The owner of the lease of 47 Park Street, which was the building above the restaurant, was Bent Nygren, a Swedish entrepreneur. Nygren had grand plans to develop the property into a timeshare but when this turned out to be impossible he decided to convert the building into a hotel. By then Nygren had become good friends with Albert and he and his wife Monique got involved with the transformation of 54 apartments into the individually styled, lavish suites that made up '47 Park Street'—and then it was agreed that we, from our basement kitchen, would run the hotel's food and beverage services by providing room service and private dining in one of the suites.

This turned out to be a great move for all involved as both businesses fed each other. One evening Charlton Heston was dining with us, as he was in town working on *A Man for All Seasons*. He happened to mention that he wasn't overly impressed with his suite at Claridge's so we took him upstairs to 47 Park Street and showed him around. He liked it a lot and a couple of days later moved in then stayed for the duration of his film project.

The private dining room, Suite 36, also attracted a high-profile clientele. Some very prestigious business meetings were held there, particularly those of the board of the General Electric Company thanks to the fact that its MD Lord Weinstock was a frequent Gavroche customer, and many incredibly important deals and decisions were made at its huge table. Antonio, the Italian manager I had met on my first day in the job back in 1971, was made *maître d'* of Suite 36 and we all knew that he must have been party to some very interesting conversations. Albert would say, 'Antonio, what are they talking about in there?'

But Antonio was very good. 'I will never tell you that,' he'd reply gravely—and he never did.

Discretion was paramount. Every year for 10 years, Le Gavroche was the venue for the Conservative Party's Christmas dinner, or for the leading members at least, as its treasurer Lord McAlpine was one of our best customers. Margaret Thatcher, Sir Geoffrey Howe, Nigel Lawson, John Major, Leon Brittan … they were all there, though whether or not they wore paper party hats I couldn't possibly say.

TOP SERVICE

From clandestine affairs to high-stakes business deals, our restaurant had to be a sanctuary for its customers. We witnessed numerous scandals and secrets, all of which stayed within the walls of Le Gavroche. Had any of us staff been so inclined we could have sold stories that would have made headlines, but we understood that our role was to create an air of privacy and relaxation for our guests. Trust was a vital part of our relationship with them, and it was something we took very seriously.

I witnessed many things that could have been life—or at least career—damaging had we spoken out, like the time a very well-known woman in her 40s and a young man in his 20s from her table slipped off to the bathroom. We had already taken orders, so had to warn the kitchen to hold their food until they got back. I had a member of staff stand guard outside the bathroom door both to redirect customers to alternative toilets and to let us know when the couple reemerged. Once they had finished whatever they had been up to and all were back at the table we served dinner as if nothing had happened—which, as far as we were concerned, it hadn't. That was the job.

Another time a regular customer, a well-known lady who was very nice, came in with a gentleman friend. This was in the middle of the '90s when we still required men to wear jackets. This gentleman had one on when he arrived but then took it off, which wasn't allowed. When asked, he refused to put it back on.

So, we stopped serving them. The woman realised why and came over to me at the bar where I was standing to have a quiet word. Thinking she'd call my bluff she said, 'What are you going to do if I remove my skirt?'

I smiled but it was Thierry Tomasin, our *sommelier* at the time, who answered. 'Jane,' he said. 'I bet you wouldn't dare.'

But he was wrong! She whipped off her skirt there and then and stood there in her tights, hands on her hips, a triumphant smile on her face. 'There!' she said. 'What are you going to do about that?!'

I smiled. 'I'm going to have a good look first,' I said. 'Then I'll ask you to put it back on!'

I got to know some of our customers very well, partly because we saw and chatted with them so often, and partly because they came to trust us in a way that well-known or well-off people often struggle with. There was a very rich Saudi prince who, from the mid-1970s on, was a very regular customer and he and I came to be very good friends. He always spent a lot of money in the restaurant, particularly on wine, though he didn't drink himself. It was only ever for those he entertained but he thought nothing of paying £4,000 for a bottle for his doctor to enjoy over their lunch.

On one occasion he arrived at the restaurant with his girlfriend—who was very different in appearance to his wife—and I showed them to their table. Nothing was out of the ordinary; he brought her in often, as was common for more of our guests than you might think. However, on this occasion, I had just left to fetch their first drink when the prince beckoned me back to their table. He looked concerned.

'Silvano,' he said. 'That table over there.' He nodded towards a table of Middle Eastern people on the far side of the room. 'You must tell them to leave immediately.'

I was a little bewildered, I don't mind saying. 'How can I do that?' I said. 'They've just ordered.'

He patted me on the shoulder. 'Don't worry,' he said. 'They'll go. Talk to the man at the head of the table. If he argues tell him to look over here.' He seemed very confident that I wouldn't have any problems.

He obviously meant business and was such a good customer and friend that I took my courage and headed over. Reaching the table I leaned in to the gentleman identified. 'I'm afraid there has been a request for your group to leave the restaurant, Sir. Would you mind leaving immediately please?'

Unsurprisingly, his first response was surprise and an indignant 'No!' So, as instructed, I told him to look over at the prince—and he nodded. 'You can blame me if you like Sir,' I said.

Immediately he started gathering his things and addressing his table. 'We must go,' he said. 'I don't like this waiter. He is arguing with me and I don't want to stay any more.' The entire party left and the prince continued on with his meal with his girlfriend.

It was a few weeks until I found out what it had all been about. Finally, he came in and I managed to ask him while he was sitting by himself, awaiting his guest. 'Why did you do that?' I asked. I wouldn't have asked other customers but we knew each other very well by then and I was comfortable to do so.

'It was my nephew,' he said. 'I was the one who told him about this place and when he visits he's stupid enough to bring one of my wives with him!' Situations like this were not uncommon, and our ability to handle them with tact and discretion was a cornerstone of our reputation.

The prince returned the favour for me once. Irene and I and some friends had had a very good but very late night out in London ... in fact, we were still out come breakfast time! We decided to go to the Hilton for breakfast and ordered a bottle of Champagne—but the waiter, apologising profusely, said he could not bring us any alcohol at that time as we weren't residents. Disappointed, we settled for a pot of coffee. However, a minute or two later a bottle of Dom Perignon arrived at our table. 'Thank you,' I said. 'But we didn't order Dom Perignon. That's too expensive.'

'It's been sent over to your table by the gentleman over there,' he said. I looked over and there was my friend the prince, who gave us a small wave and a nod. We certainly enjoyed those bubbles! Many years later, when I eventually retired from Le Gavroche in 2008, he stopped over in his personal plane, which was en route from Paris to Washington, to sit down and have a last meal with me in Le Gavroche.

In 1991, Albert decided to step back from Gavroche to concentrate on his consultancy work. At this time I too was starting to enjoy spreading my wings. Though I was still very much present at Gavroche for most sittings, I sometimes worked with Albert on projects, which meant travelling across the UK and sometimes abroad. I would also sometimes get 'lent out' for private engagements. During this time, I was honoured to serve several distinguished guests outside the restaurant, including Queen Elizabeth as a guest in Lord Weinstock's home, and at another private engagement French President Jacques Chirac who rather to my dismay preferred beer to wine.

Michel Roux Jr took over at Le Gavroche. He was—and still is—as innovative as his father Albert and uncle Michel Snr, and he brought a fresh perspective to the menu. Under his leadership, we made some significant changes that were ahead of their time, including adding to the menu lighter, healthier dishes that appealed to a new generation of diners.

However, these changes did not sit well with Michelin, and that same year we were downgraded to two stars. Despite this, we remained philosophical. The Michelin guide was important, but it did not define us. The restaurant continued to flourish despite the loss of the third Michelin star and we were proud to remain true to our values, focusing on quality, consistency, and customer satisfaction. Our patrons came for the experience, the ambience and the impeccable service. We knew Michel Jr's approach was right for the restaurant and our people continued to flock to Le Gavroche, appreciating the fresh, contemporary approach.

The 1990s were not such a prosperous time for the UK and we, like most businesses, suffered as a result of the economic downturn. However, we introduced a new set lunch menu of three courses with a half bottle of wine, which became a great value proposition and kept our dining room bustling. It offered exceptional value without compromising on quality, ensuring that we remained busy even in tough times. This made the difference between going under and surviving to see in the new millennium. This was a testament to our ability to adapt and thrive in challenging times.

We also did well because of our location, and business diners continued to visit—though as the economy changed so did the nature of the businesses in the Upper Brook Street area. When we arrived in 1981 there were many people in the oil industry, then in the '90s, all the property people took over. By the beginning of the new millennium, we were sometimes full of hedge fund workers. But though the nature of the street changed Le Gavroche stayed busy. It was a destination in itself.

Such was the love for and loyalty towards Gavroche expressed by some of the customers some almost became part of the Le Gavroche family. Any staff member who worked at the restaurant in the '90s would remember the guest who always insisted on having a small pile of chopped fresh ginger on the side of his plate and then eating with chopsticks, or 'Mr Cappucino,' a doctor who would end each meal with five or six strong coffees before heading back to work.

Another such guest was an elderly member of the very rich and influential Whitbread family. This gentleman lived around the corner from the restaurant and lunched with us every weekday at 12:30 sharp, almost without fail, for 18 years. He would sometimes come on his own, sometimes with a guest, and always start with the Soufflé Suissesse then follow with fish or fois gras.

However, as the years passed he sadly started to develop dementia and became increasingly confused. As his illness progressed he would sometimes arrive for lunch at 12:30, only to return again at two, unaware he had already eaten. Of course, we treated him with kindness and respect, understanding the importance of maintaining his dignity, but I was personally in a dilemma about this: did I serve him again so as not to embarrass him? I did this a few times but was worried that his family might think we were taking advantage, as all his bills were sent to them to pay.

Sure enough, his nephew phoned us to ask how his uncle could be having two lunches in a day. So we came to a new arrangement whereby we would put him in a taxi at the end of lunch to be sure he would get home to where there would be someone to care for him. He would eat lunch, I would put him in the taxi and pay the driver, and he'd be on his way home.

But then one day, as his illness progressed further, we encountered a new problem. I put him in a taxi but half an hour later he came back in. 'I need more money for the taxi,' he said. I went out to talk to the driver, concerned the gentleman was being ripped off.

The driver was apologetic. 'He's had me taking him all over the place,' he said. 'We've even been back to your old place in Lower Sloane Street. He's clocked up ten pounds so far.' I gave him £15 and told him to take the gentleman straight home.

Eventually, the family moved him to their country estate in Bedfordshire—but we would still see him here for lunch on occasion, as he would ask constantly. He'd arrive in a chauffeur-driven car that would thankfully wait for him and take him straight back again after. His family knew how well we'd looked after him though and were very appreciative.

This story is just one of many I could tell that go some way to illustrate that Le Gavroche was more than just a restaurant, more even than a top-class, world-famous, multi-award winning restaurant stuffed to the rafters with the rich, famous and powerful. It was an institution, a legend and, to some, a home-from-home.

To me, it was all those things and more. Yet still, alongside the rich and sometimes all-encompassing way of life at Le Gavroche, my career horizons were expanding further than I could ever have imagined.

Albert Roux & his team

With David Galetti and Emmanuel Landre

Team picture in front of Le Gavroche

With Albert Roux & Steven Doherty

With Albert & Michel Roux

ws out

ears of service

nuel Landré, who has
years, working his way
sistant Manager. Giraldin
g "I wouldn't leave Le

Silvano Giraldin will hand over the reins to Emmanuel Landré (left) in September

2008 on my retirement

le Gavroche, new team with David Galetti, Emmanuel Landre, Rachel Humphrey and Enrico Molino

CHAPTER 4: CULINARY HEIGHTS

By the time we entered the new millennium my career was even more exciting than it had ever been … and perhaps a little more fun too! In the 1980s, my work started to take me beyond the borders of the UK, working alongside the Roux brothers on consultancy projects that would shape some of the finest hotels, restaurants and hospitality establishments around the world—all while maintaining my role front of house at Le Gavroche, which Jean Claude took very good care of in my absence.

The consultancy work wasn't just about shaping or enhancing restaurants; it was about crafting experiences that would leave a lasting impression on guests, and I'm proud to say that every project we worked on was a success. From the '80s, through the '90s and into the 2000s and beyond I worked on a fantastic array of consultancies, in many different capacities—some from the beginning, some only in the weeks leading up to opening, some at the request of the brothers and some with me leading the way. What's more, these projects presented some incredible opportunities for me and my family.

The first outside project I was asked to contribute to was The Waterside Inn in Santa Barbara which, like the original three Michelin star restaurant in Bray, would become synonymous with culinary excellence. In 1984 I travelled business class to California to train the restaurant's front-of-the-house staff before it opened—and what a trip that was. I remember sitting on the plane feeling like life had suddenly gone up a notch. It was incredibly exciting, not just because I was getting to travel to a fabulous destination but also because of the trust invested in me: if I needed outside confirmation that I was doing a great job at Le Gavroche, this was it.

That same year I travelled back to Santa Barbara for a second time to help with a black-and-white ball to raise funds for Ronald Reagan's re-election campaign. This event stands out in my memory, not just because of the array of Hollywood stars all in one place, but also because it was one of the best services I had ever managed—and not necessarily because of my own talents! The staff hired to wait the tables were all actors, brought in through Reagan's connections, and each played their role perfectly by following my instructions to the letter.

Another fascinating chapter began in 1987. Not only was that the year that, to my immense pride, I was made a director of Le Gavroche this was also the year I started work on a fabulous project at the behest of Toufic Aboukhater, a wealthy Lebanese businessman and frequent patron of Le Gavroche.

Aboukhater had bought the Isola 2000 ski resort, in a fantastic location at an altitude of 2000 meters yet just an hour's drive from Nice and Cannes. He wanted to make Isola 2000 the absolute best of its kind—and he asked Roux Consultancies to help from the start. Albert designed the hotel whilst standing on the bare dirt at its intended spot, on the back of a menu—'We want the kitchens here, the dining room here, the terrace here'—and from that point on it was built from scratch.

At first, we had been sceptical about Aboukhater's intended timeline. In the spring of 1987 Michel Jnr and I had stood overlooking the bare bones of a building site, doubting it would ever be built by Christmas of that year, as was the plan. Michel Jnr oversaw the development and I accompanied him on a number of trips, making plans for the restaurant and everything and everybody it would need. in December 1987 just eight or so months after building had commenced we were back there, overseeing the finishing touches as it prepared to open.

If I tell you that Gordon Ramsay was one of the junior chefs at Isola 2000 you'll have a good idea of the calibre of the place. It was a huge success ... and thankfully I got to enjoy some of the fruits of my labour. For a number of years, I was needed to continue front-of-house training and manage key personnel like Jean Claude Breton and Enzo Casini to ensure the highest standards were maintained ... and I was lucky enough to be able to take my family with me. Every school holiday we would arrive at Nice airport and then head up to the mountains for a week or two of skiing and spending quality time together. The hotel provided an apartment for Irene and the boys and I was able to balance work with leisure. Sometimes they would join me in the main hotel restaurant for a fantastic meal at the start of the dinner service—and on more than one occasion Gordon, still a young chef but already clearly very talented, cooked them omelettes to order. The boys still remember those omelettes … they must have been good! These personal touches and the opportunity to travel with my family made consultancy work even more rewarding.

The 1990s saw me working in a cold climate once more, at Le Rond Point des Pistes in Courchevel 1850 for the 1992 Winter Olympics in the French Alps. This project was particularly significant as it served as the headquarters for government officials during the games. Of course, as always we were expected to deliver a very high-quality experience— and we delivered. Again, my family were there with me for some of the time and it was a very rewarding experience.

Many more prestigious consultancies on the continent followed, quite a number of which came about thanks to Le Gavroche, the standards it showcased and the connections made through its patrons. There was The Grand Hotel and Restaurant in Amsterdam; Bertie's restaurant in the Baltimore Hotel in Paris; and Il Cortile restaurant at Hotel Castille in Paris.

One standout project from this time was further afield: The Point at Saranac Lake in upstate New York, a former Rockefeller summer retreat turned luxury resort. By this point, I was in my 50s and had worked with the Roux brothers for 25 years, and they continued to be as good to me then as they had been on my first day.

The Point was incredibly luxurious and known for its exclusivity and serene ambience. In the initial stages, the project had involved transforming 13 cabins into fabulous retreats with a main cabin for dining, but by the time I got there, it was already up and running and achieving great things. Ran day-to-day by Bill McNamee, another very talented chef who had at one time worked at Le Gavroche, it had a unique concept of away-from-it-all peace and simplicity where guests could truly disconnect from the outside world. Guests, who were often very high-profile, consistently voted it among the best in the United States, a testament to the exceptional service and ambience created by Bill and his team.

I wasn't sent there to work, not really. I had very little to do and this trip was more of a perk, a chance for me to enjoy the resort's offerings while admiring Bill's exceptional food and management. My family joined me on this adventure too, though whereas Irene and I enjoyed each fantastic communal meal in the main cabin, where we would chat to the other 20 or so guests, the boys usually continued racing about on jet skis on the lake and then ate in our cabin. Whichever, we all had a wonderful time and I was incredibly proud to be able to provide my family with such unique experiences.

Though I got a huge amount of satisfaction from my career in itself, it's undeniable that it also gave me fabulous opportunities to develop my hobbies that I doubt I would have had access to otherwise.

I discovered skiing when I worked the seasons as a young man then managed to go on a few occasions through the '70s and early to mid-'80s. Then in 1987—just as we started work on Isola 2000—Irene and I bought an apartment at Les Arcs 1800 in Savoie, France. This was a perfect winter escape, and we enjoyed numerous skiing trips which were made even better when a ski lift opened linking Les Arcs with La Plagne, offering access to over 700 km of ski slopes. This area, known as Paradiski, provided endless opportunities for adventure and exploration.

With our own apartment in Les Arcs and regular stays at Isola 2000, skiing became a cornerstone of family life. Alexander and Sebastian became expert skiers—and now my eldest grandchildren have started on the nursery slopes too. We still have the apartment at Les Arcs, though the boys visit more than Irene and I do now. It's more than just a property; it's a symbol of family unity and shared adventure.

Shooting was another sport that became a lifelong love thanks to Le Gavroche. I was introduced to it by Michel Snr and Albert but it was Antonio who really got me hooked. An avid shooter himself, he invited me along to his small shoot, a walk-up event without beaters, and I learned to love the exercise, the camaraderie, and just being in the great outdoors … no small thing to those of us who spent our working lives in dining rooms and hot kitchens.

Shooting quickly became a significant part of my life. Thanks to friends and connections made through work I found myself very lucky to be invited to shoot across the UK and Europe. These included prestigious invitations from the Rapeneau family at Chateau de Bligny, Lord Sharman in Spain, John Apthorp in Yorkshire, Glenn McCorquodale in Camfield, Terry Smith at Loyton Lodge in Devon, Mark Walford in Herefordshire and in Spain, and Andrew Vartan at Elton Hall, among many others. I never would have had experiences such as these were it not for the great generosity of the various hosts.

For me, one of the great highlights of my shooting adventures was the annual trip to Paul Lock's shooting ground in East Sussex, sponsored by Mumm Champagne, which was always brilliant fun—but one trip was particularly memorable. Though we were staying in the same excellent hotel as usual, on the second night we were all invited to dinner at Albert's house near Petworth. It was a fantastic gathering of stellar chefs: Paul Bocuse, Bernard Loiseau, Jean Lameloise, Gaston Lenotre, Pierre Romeijer, Jean Pierre Vigato, Albert of course—and then me.

It was a fairly rowdy evening as you might imagine, and plenty of fantastic food and wine was enjoyed by all. However, at some point in the evening, Paul Bocuse decided we needed more wine ... and persuaded me to go with him to raid Albert's wine cellar.

Down in the cool depths, surrounded by a lifetime's accumulation of some of the world's finest wines, Paul poked around and suddenly emerged triumphant, holding a bottle aloft.

'Aha!' he proclaimed. 'This'll do!' I peered hazily at the label. It was a bottle of 1971 Domaine de la Romanee-Conti —an extremely rare find that today would sell for around £20,000.

'You can't!' I laughed—but he was going to. Paul headed back to the others and by the time I arrived the bottle was being uncorked and Albert, to his eternal credit, was laughing along with the rest of them. That wine was indeed delicious—

though I'm not sure any of us were in a state to fully appreciate it!

Throughout the 2000s I continued to travel further afield, to White Barn Inn in Kennebunkport, Maine, and memorably to the tropical paradise of Hotel Beau Rivage Ile Maurice in Mauritius, where Irene, Alexander, Sebastian and I saw in the new millennium on New Year's Eve 1999.

This period brought new challenges, particularly with ICMI Consultancies in Scotland. Our projects with them included Inverlochy Castle in Fort William, a historic hotel where our expertise helped maintain its grandeur; Greywalls near Muirfield Golf course in Gullane, known for its elegant charm and excellent service; Inverlodge at Loch Inver; Rockpool Reserve in Inverness; Cromlix in Dunblane; and Crossbasket near Glasgow. Each project required our trademark meticulous attention to detail, which for me meant anything from curating wine lists to training staff, and together as Roux Consultancies, we helped them achieve very high standards of service and hospitality. I remember my time at Greywalls particularly fondly because Irene and I stayed there for a couple of months so I could train all the front-of-the-house staff, and we had a lovely time. I would work in the morning but often in the afternoon my time was my own, and each night Irene and I would eat in the restaurant and find out how the new menus were coming along.

There were more, including La Torretta del Lago in Houston, Texas, with Gareth Donovan as restaurant manager, and Le Gavroche Des Tropiques inside La Voile d'Or in Mauritius with Monica and David Galetti. Country by country we continued to make significant contributions to the hospitality industry. There were projects closer to home too, for Chez Roux, Albert's own consultancy business. My expertise was sought at various prestigious venues like Roux at the Landau Langham Hotel in London, Roux at Parliament Square in London, Brasserie Roux in the Sofitel St James, Glyndebourne, Henley Festival, The Gatsby Club and The Lawn at Wimbledon, and The Jockey Club at Cheltenham, Newmarket, and Epsom.

But in 2008 I turned 60—and it was time for me to retire from Le Gavroche, as I had always intended. This of course was a huge milestone. Having dedicated myself through long hours and demanding schedules for 37 years I physically couldn't do it any more.

When you work in service, day to day, it's pretty tough. Weekdays would always start in the Gavroche head office on Wandsworth Road, not far from where I live. I would stay there for an hour or so, overseeing the accountants and invoices that I had taken home from the restaurant the night before, and signing cheques and papers. Then I'd head over to the restaurant for about 11 o'clock where I'd check if everything was OK. I'd take lunch with the staff, though at the management table where we would discuss any problems that had arisen. Quarter to 12 would see me briefing the staff —and then it would be lunch service.

By around half past three to four o'clock I would head home to refresh and see my family for an hour or so ... though very often that meant falling asleep as I tried to read the newspaper. And then it would be back to work from 6:30 until about one o'clock in the morning. My days were punishing.

For around 20 years we had opened only on weekdays, but in 2001, when No 47 Park Street was sold and we lost the private dining room, we decided to open on a Saturday night to replace the lost revenue. Though we weren't open for lunch on Saturdays we did staff training in the afternoons. This meant my days off were now, like the rest of the staff, Sundays plus an additional day during the week which wasn't as restful as a full weekend—and on the days I worked I needed to be first in and last out.

It was hard, but I coped—thanks to Irene. I was seeing my children for just an hour or so in the afternoons and sleeping in a chair for some of that! She did everything so that I could dedicate myself to my work.

It's undeniable that working in hospitality is a vocation. You can only do it for the enjoyment you give to the customers. We front-of-house staff are merchants of happiness. If I give happiness to a customer, it's happiness to me. Their smile and their thanks are what make it all worthwhile. But, much as I loved it, daily front-of-house work was for a younger man than me, and I needed to step back.

My farewell from Le Gavroche was celebrated with two grand events honouring my contributions and the relationships I had built over the years. Michel Jnr and Albert closed Le Gavroche one evening and invited 70 or 80 of our top customers for a fantastic evening. But there were still more friends to celebrate with so on another day they threw a cocktail party for two or three hundred people. So many came to say goodbye, which meant the world to me.

One of the best things that came about because of my retirement was … my Chelsea FC season ticket, which a group of friends clubbed together to buy as a leaving gift. My connection to Chelsea FC began in the mid-1970s when Irene and I bought an apartment near Stamford Bridge. From the rooftop, I could watch the games and this sparked a lifelong passion.

Over the years I became friends with several Chelsea players and club officials, deepening my bond with the team —but I had never owned a season ticket. Since retirement, however, I'm proud to say I've never missed a home game. Like shooting, for me, football is about more than the sport: it's being part of a community and a deep-rooted passion that brings me immense joy.

Even after retiring from the day-to-day operations of Le Gavroche, I continued with a significant load of consultancy work with Chez Roux, including involvement with some of those mentioned above. My expertise was still in demand and by working I keep my brain ticking over, stay connected to the industry I love … and also keep the wolf from the door!

Once retired, I took on some personal consultancies too: Eureka Executive Search, where I used my extensive network to help identify top industry talent; Redleaf Communications, which I advised on PR and marketing strategies; Just Great Wines and Chateau Cabezac, where I helped market and sell fine wines; the luxurious Villa Giuseppina at Lake Como; Toto's Restaurant in London; and Harry's Bar in Beirut.

TOP SERVICE

To be able to play a role in all these iconic establishments was always a pleasure—and it brought me satisfaction and rewards beyond my career.

Les Arts de la Table function

Academie Culinaire de France in the UK before it change the name to Royal Academy of Culinary Arts

Gold Service Scholarship 2016 Awards ceremony

With the Queen Elisabeth II

Shooting dinner in Albert House with Paul Bocuse, Patrick Millet, Pierre Romeijer, Jean Lameloise & Philippe Pascal

Camfield Shoot 28-11-2009

Shooting day

Chasse au Chateau de Bligny

CHAPTER 5: GOOD WORK & REWARDS

As I hope I've made clear so far, my career in hospitality has brought me immense satisfaction and joy. But I didn't just enjoy the day-to-day challenges and rewards of my job; I also found great fulfilment in mentoring and training staff.

From early on I knew that, as I had benefitted so much from the industry, one day I would like to be able to give something back. As I climbed the career ladder and was able to view my profession from a wider perspective, I became aware of a gaping need for ways to encourage and nurture talent within front-of-house staff. And so, with the memory of signors Trevini and Generali and numerous other generous and talented people I had met along my way, I set my mind to doing something about it.

My efforts towards this began in the 1980s as I watched what others were doing. Inspired by French culinary organisations, industry leaders including Albert and Michel Snr had identified the need for a UK body dedicated to promoting excellence in cooking, and this vision materialised as The Royal Academy of Culinary Arts (RACA). This was followed in 1983 by The Roux Scholarship—the brothers' own brainchild and the UK industry's most acclaimed chef competition which still runs to this day and ranks among the best in the world.

Having admired their efforts, I got together with Jean Pierre Durantet—by then manager at La Tante Claire—and a few other like-minded professionals to create a similar organisation for front-of-house staff. This would be aimed at raising their profile and value, particularly as the industry shifted from tableside service to dishes plated in the kitchen; we were in danger of being seen as simply plate carriers.

After a lot of discussions, meetings and fund-raising efforts Les Arts de la Table was launched. It was a success and eventually merged into RACA, broadening the body's scope and impact—and it has continued to evolve significantly over the years. However, its basic aim remains the same: to elevate the standards of cooking and front-of-house service and to create a platform for professionals to network, gain recognition, and share their knowledge and skills.

RACA's commitment to fostering talent can be seen in its annual Awards of Excellence. These awards, patronized by King Charles III, recognise outstanding young chefs, front-of-house staff, and pastry chefs, providing them with platforms to further their professional development. The competition includes various stages, from quarterfinals to finals, and assesses participants on multiple criteria, including practical skills and customer service. The Awards of Excellence are among the most prestigious available to young professionals in the industry and they have helped countless young professionals gain recognition and further their careers.

Additionally, every four years, RACA holds the Master of Culinary Arts (MCA) awards, which recognise the best craftspeople in the industry, setting an extremely high standard for chefs, pastry chefs and restaurant managers. The rigorous judging process evaluates contestants on practical skills, customer service and knowledge, ensuring that only the most skilled professionals are honoured. What was especially rewarding was that we in the UK led the way when it came to holding the MCA in service. When the French saw what we were doing they too added a service award to their equivalent, the MOF. Of that, I am very proud.

For me, a very important element of the awards, particularly the Awards of Excellence, is the opportunity for these budding young professionals to get together. Hospitality workers, working long hours in sometimes remote locations, can get quite isolated and rarely have time to meet others in the industry outside their own establishment. In getting together at these events they make connections and become a family.

These networking opportunities were further enhanced when, in 2012, I joined forces with a few industry stalwarts like Alastair Storey, Willy Bauer, Edward Griffiths and Sergio Rebecchi to develop the Gold Service Scholarship. This initiative provides exceptional training opportunities for front-of-house staff who are already demonstrating excellence. The scholarship, patronized by the late Queen Elizabeth II, joins with top culinary schools and industry leaders to offer development experiences to young professionals. We send them to the Lausanne Catering School (EHL Hospitality

Business School) in Switzerland, one of the best of its kind in the world for a tailor-made course, as well as on visits to vineyards, top international hotels and restaurants, and for a host of other experiences, all to further their education in the industry.

I find helping young professionals in these ways incredibly rewarding. For nearly 40 years now, I have watched them enter our programmes, receive awards, make connections and climb the ladder, some to the very top of the industry. It makes me very proud, but I must repeat that there are many others working hard too, from the individuals attending the meetings or judging the awards to organisations providing us with venues free of charge or inviting our young people to experience and learn from their own practice.

My commitment to giving back also extends beyond the hospitality industry. For the past seven years, I have been actively involved with Clink, a charity that provides kitchen and front-of-house training to prison inmates with the aim of improving their employment prospects on their release with a chance at a career in hospitality.

My efforts within the industry have not gone unnoticed, and I've been the recipient of a number of top awards over the years. The most prestigious of these are the two Cateys awards, nicknamed the 'Hospitality Industry Oscars': the Special Achievement award in 2000 and the Lifetime Achievement award in 2013; both times I won I was so surprised that I had no prepared speech and could only blurt out a few words of thanks. I was humbled and overwhelmed to be singled out in such a way, but certainly recovered enough to celebrate well afterwards. Both awards have pride of place on my mantlepiece,

Other notable accolades that I've won over the years include the Best Maitre D' by *Observer Magazine* in 1991, Restaurant Manager of the Year 2007 from *Restaurant Magazine*, plus awards from Dom Perignon, Moet & Chandon, Harpers & Queen and *Restaurant Magazine.*

As a result of my experience and profile within the industry, I've also been asked to present at various events over the years, including the MAD Symposium in Copenhagen in 2014. I consider this to be one of my proudest achievements. I made no money from it of course but it was very good for my ego! I've also been featured in numerous magazine and newspaper articles. However, as grateful as I am for the awards and recognition, I strongly believe that true success lies not in personal accolades but in the ability to uplift and inspire others.

And so, to the future: despite the significant progress made in the hospitality industry over the past 50 years, there is still much work to be done, particularly in gaining government support for initiatives that have so far been funded by goodwill. There is a huge contrast between the French and English approaches to supporting the hospitality industry: France provides substantial government support, while England doesn't even have a dedicated Minister for Tourism or any apprenticeship programmes. This is why today, despite the hard work put in by so many and the progress that has been made, I remain actively involved in all these initiatives and organisations. However, it's also important for us to bring younger people into leadership roles in these bodies in order to maintain relevance, growth and momentum.

We have achieved so much and I think Trevini and Generali would be proud of me—yet there is still much to be done. I intend to continue to do as much as I can for as long as I am able. The hospitality industry has given me so much, and my efforts are focused on uplifting and inspiring others. The awards and recognition are meaningful, but the real satisfaction comes from knowing that I've made a difference in the lives of many.

Skying with the family

Christmas dinner 1989 Isola 2000 Diva Hotel

Saranac Lake with the family and Bill Mc Namee

Beau Rivage Hotel in Mauritius with Irene, Philippe Requin, Giselle and Michel Roux

Beau Rivage Hotel new year 2000

La Voile d'Or in Mauritius with David, Irene & Monica Galetti

Harry's Bar in Beirut

Fabulous Cateys 2013

Westminster College

Lunch at the Waterside Inn with Irene and Alain Roux

Some of the best recognition

CHAPTER 6: THE JOURNEY CONTINUES

Looking back on my career and life, I'm filled with pride and gratitude. The journey has been remarkably rich, full of unforgettable experiences, challenges and achievements that have shaped who I am today: from my early days in Padua, helping on the family farm and making decisions that I didn't then grasp would be momentous; to my invaluable time learning, learning, learning in high-end hotels around Europe; and then my time at Le Gavroche, which was nothing short of extraordinary. Serving the Queen, organising high-profile events, and mentoring future industry leaders were highlights. But the true essence of my role was creating an environment where guests felt special and taken care of.

In particular, I will always carry with me the remarkable, heartwarming, and often funny times at Le Gavroche, moments that defined the collective experience of those of us who were lucky enough to work there. I have had the privilege of working with incredibly talented people and making lifelong friends. Through the challenges we faced, our commitment to excellence never wavered, and I'm proud that our efforts were recognised.

Le Gavroche was more than just a job; it was a family. The camaraderie among the staff, the passion for perfection and the shared joy of creating unforgettable dining experiences made every day special. Being part of the restaurant's journey from Chelsea to Mayfair, witnessing its rise to culinary stardom, and becoming known as 'Mr Gavroche' was an honour. Serving some of the world's most distinguished guests and seeing young talents grow into exceptional professionals are memories I will cherish forever. The restaurant was not just a place to eat but an institution where culinary excellence met impeccable service. The standards we set, the innovations we introduced, and the experiences we created have left an indelible mark on the culinary world. Le Gavroche closed its doors for good in 2024, marking the end of an era. Yet, its spirit lives on in the memories of those who dined there, the staff who worked there, and the culinary world it influenced. I am honoured to have been a part of this legacy.

And now? Even though my day-to-day involvement with consultancy projects has ended, I still keep my hand in professionally. My work in maintaining the highest possible standards in hospitality at prestigious events like Wimbledon, Cheltenham, Epsom and Newmarket keeps me connected to the industry. But perhaps the most rewarding aspect of my work nowadays is my continuing involvement with the Royal Academy of Culinary Arts and The Gold Service Scholarship, which allows me to continue contributing to the development of service as a career, a passion that remains close to my heart.

At the beginning and end of it all family has always been my anchor. Irene remains my rock, having supported me through every high and low for over 50 years. Her support and understanding allowed me to focus on my work and excel. Our family was and still is my source of strength, and their happiness was reflected in my work. Our sons Alexander and Sebastian continue to be a great source of pride and joy —emotions that have only grown thanks to the arrival of our grandchildren James, Jessica, Noah and the newly-hatched Louis. Our family gatherings, especially the recent reunion with over 30 much-loved relatives at our holiday home in Normandy, are moments I treasure deeply. Balancing work and family life has never been easy, but the love and support from Irene and our boys made it all possible.

Irene and I continue to share a passion for dining out which we now have more time to indulge. We regularly visit our favourite local restaurants as well as high-end establishments such as Gordon Ramsay's Royal Hospital, Alain Ducasse at the Dorchester and Waterside Inn at Bray—which is now expertly run by Michel Snr's son Alain, and the only restaurant in the world, outside France, to have retained three stars for over 39 years. These outings are not just about enjoying great food but also about experiencing the excellence in service and hospitality, which continues to inspire me. As I look forward to the future, I'm excited about the possibilities that lie ahead. Continuing to work on selected projects, pursuing my hobbies, and enjoying time with my family are my priorities.

My life so far has been remarkable and I'm eager to see what the next chapter will bring.

Family lunch at The Savoy grill

Last dinner in Gavroche with all the family

In Le Gavroche kitchen with Michel Roux & my grand children Jessy, Noah, James

Irene with all my grand children

EPILOGUE: INVISIBLE HEROES— SILVANO'S GUIDE TO SUPERB SERVICE

In the competitive world of fine dining, our efforts to provide impeccable service at Le Gavroche gave us an edge. Ours became the gold standard that many aspired to. Every day, at every service, for every table, we aimed not just to meet but to far exceed every guest's expectations.

It goes without saying that the food at Le Gavroche was absolutely fantastic and very largely unrivalled. You can't have a fantastic restaurant without fantastic food. But when fabulous food was combined with exemplary service and world-class wines ... a wonderful meal was transformed into an unforgettable experience.

Front-of-house staff serve as the vital link between the kitchen and the customer, ensuring that both are satisfied. They are delivering what the customers want, whilst also keeping the kitchen staff happy so they can perform to the best of their abilities. If you don't have that fantastic service in between, then the experience that the customer receives is not going to be what it should be.

Achieving Excellence

This next statement might sound contradictory, but bear with me: part of Le Gavroche's success lay in its ability to make guests feel at home while offering them the ultimate luxury. At Le Gavroche, creating a homely yet luxurious environment was key to its success. The ambience was carefully crafted to balance elegance and comfort. And it was the incredibly attentive yet unobtrusive service that made guests feel both special and at ease.

Of course, before aiming for greatness the basics need to be in place. A warm welcome sets the tone for the entire dining experience. Greet guests with eye contact and a genuine smile and make them feel valued from the moment they walk in. Very early in my career, I learned an important lesson from a top waiter at Hotel Negresco in Nice: a smile will get you a long way (and often, out of trouble too). He had a huge, infectious smile himself, and a fantastic attitude, and he always said: 'If you don't know something—just smile. You'll get away with it!'

What else? Appearance is important. Staff should always be clean, tidy and dressed appropriately; these things contribute significantly to the overall impression. Familiarity with the menu is essential. Staff should be able to describe each dish, suggest drink pairings and cater to dietary restrictions confidently. And taking customers' orders is of course central to everything. We had a great system at Le

Gavroche for always getting it right. We started with the host of the table then went round the table clockwise and wrote them in order. That way, when the waiters brought the food to the table they didn't have to ask who ordered what, they already knew.

So, get the basics right. But what then takes acceptable service to exceptional service is the ability to personalise the dining experience. To achieve this, staff need to maintain a delicate balance of attentiveness, knowledge, sensitivity and discretion.

During my time in service, I was known for having a very good memory. I made a point of being able to recall names. People love it when they're recognised, even (or perhaps especially) celebrities, in a restaurant environment at least. I will always say that a famous person's favourite restaurant is usually one in which they are known because they get the level of service they consider they deserve.

I also took note of important milestones celebrated, customers' significant relationships, their preferences ... and their peculiarities too. This personal touch made regulars feel valued and appreciated, which in turn encouraged their loyalty.

If you can, watch carefully as you approach customers, particularly those new to the restaurant, to gauge the level of formality each requires on that occasion. Some guests enjoy a more formal interaction, particularly when entertaining business contacts, while others prefer a relaxed atmosphere. Gauge the level of formality each guest prefers and adjust your approach accordingly.

Don't forget the importance of discretion, however. If you're paying attention and getting to know your customers then you will get to know a lot about them ... and so you should also take note of what not to say, particularly when it comes to romantic relationships, business connections and so on.

There were of course times when I couldn't remember a name, even if I knew the face. I had a little way to dodge that problem: I would send a junior member of staff, who wouldn't be expected to know, on ahead to ask. I would listen in discreetly then approach, arms open wide, and greet them by name.

Then, after the all-important greeting, it's vital to get them that first drink right and to ensure that it's a great one.

Once a table has first drinks and orders have been taken it's all about being attentive. Guests should not have to ask for anything. At Le Gavroche, it was important that we anticipated their every need, whatever that might be—a glass of water, new cutlery, more drinks.

However, excellent service must also be invisible. The goal is to be attentive without being intrusive and guests must feel looked after without being constantly interrupted. The way to achieve this is to monitor the customer very carefully and pay attention to every small detail so that you know what they want before they know themselves.

I would tell my staff to always focus on the area between the customer's head and the table, which helps in anticipating needs without making guests feel watched. Read their body language and facial expressions to anticipate their needs.

Refill their drinks before they ask, replace used utensils promptly, and be ready to address any concerns.

However, just to make things even harder, though each guest deserves your full attention, excellent front-of-house staff will always maintain an awareness of the entire dining room to catch any potential issues. Watch individuals carefully but also stay aware of the room as a whole.

But no matter the level of excellence you achieve no person, no team, no restaurant can avoid coming across the occasional problem or unhappy customer. And how you address these situations is often the difference between a customer who complains about you to all and sundry—and someone who sings your praises all over town.

At Le Gavroche, we had a system whereby a plate of food that had not been finished must be left for senior staff such as myself to clear. That way we could ask if there had been any problems and address them immediately, while at the same time showing the individual their feedback is valued. If necessary, the chef could come out and address the problem —guests appreciate direct communication from the kitchen, especially when an apology is offered for any mistakes. This proactive approach not only resolved problems quickly but often left customers even happier than if there had been no problem at all!

The Foundations of Wine Knowledge

A significant part of front-of-house service is knowledge of wine. Michel was very generous in helping to further my own wine education, not least because it was a personal passion of his; he had a very good palate and had he not been a top chef he would have been a very successful wine merchant. I have always tried to pay that forward by supporting the wine knowledge of my staff, and of course, it only helps the customer experience when they are attended to by someone who knows what they are talking about. At the very least, learning to identify common wine flaws, such as cork taint or oxidation, ensures that only the best wines are served to guests.

So even if a staff member is not a *sommelier*, it's very desirable for them to develop a good palate and to be able to make recommendations. This requires constant tasting and learning, both on the job and through formal tastings. Understanding wine enhances the dining experience, allowing staff to pair wines with dishes that complement each other perfectly.

Wine knowledge is an art that requires dedication, continuous learning and a passion for tasting. Constantly experimenting with different wines is the most effective way to develop the palate. Each bottle opened is an opportunity to learn and refine understanding.

You can't beat professional development such as attending tastings and wine events and visiting vineyards for really broadening wine expertise, however. These provide exposure to a wide range of wines and insights from industry experts. Visits to vineyards are a real treat, and advance wine appreciation almost beyond measure. Understanding wine production by seeing the process firsthand and talking to winemakers really deepens appreciation and knowledge. Also, seek out mentors and learn from them. Guidance from experienced *sommeliers* and wine professionals is just invaluable. Their expertise can accelerate learning and inspire.

And, as with everything else, accept mistakes and learn from them. When a customer disagrees with the assessment of a wine, use it as an opportunity to reassess and learn—and recognise that everyone has their own tastes. Also, encourage feedback from customers about their wine choices. This not only improves service but also enhances wine knowledge through diverse opinions.

Caring for Staff

But there is a bottom line to all the above. You can have as many techniques and systems for excellent service as you like but if a team isn't made up of the right people—and if they're not happy in themselves and their job—then it can't be achieved. Attitude is everything. I only hire staff that are proactive, enthusiastic and eager to learn and grow. Skills can be taught, but dedication and a positive attitude are what is most important.

With the right people, you can then foster a culture of continuous improvement. I took great pride in training and guiding young staff members, not just so they performed to the best of their ability but also so they could progress and feel fulfilled. Training went on every day, but every Saturday there was an hour before dinner dedicated to it. If there was a new dish the chef would talk us through it and everyone would take notes, then they'd try it. Or we'd go through any mistakes that had recently occurred, or we'd discuss ways of improving anything that needed it.

I would only take on staff who would commit to staying for at least a year so that they could benefit from this, and so we could benefit from the consistency. However, I would also recommend to most that after a couple of years that they moved on if they were ambitious; senior positions at Le Gavroche became available rarely as for us it was a great working environment.

My approach to leadership was one of support and encouragement, and I strongly encouraged collaboration. At Le Gavroche, particularly in the early days when we were all young and constantly striving to innovate, this created an environment where everyone could thrive. A supportive and collaborative environment meant we were all working towards the same aim: providing the best possible dining experience for the guests.

That's not to say that there was no hierarchy, or that I didn't keep staff in line: quite the contrary. I was very tough on my staff. I demanded hard work and excellence— but was also very fair. What's more, I never asked for anything that I hadn't done myself, and I was always was behind them ready to offer support if needed. I was watching to see if somebody was going under ... and if they were I'd be in there to rescue them. That was my duty.

One thing that was also very important to me was the happiness of my staff. It was vital that they were content and felt valued if they were to present a welcoming front to customers. What's more, if they're not happy they leave, and high staff turnover can disrupt the consistency and quality of service, so maintaining staff morale and well-being is a priority. Ensure staff are well-fed, well-rested and appreciated. A positive work environment translates into better service. The Roux brothers certainly understood the importance of looking after their team—I was very well looked after throughout my career with them—as evidenced by the fact that I stayed with them for over 40 years!

Staff need to be settled at home too. My experience in Paris taught me that. For customers to be happy, front-of-house staff need to be happy. Chefs and other kitchen staff don't have that problem; hidden away in the kitchen, they can still do their jobs even if they're miserable. Front of house cannot. If they're struggling for any reason it's obvious to everyone, and the customers do not get the experience they come for.

Notable Alumni

The success of Le Gavroche and our approach to running a restaurant and nurturing staff is reflected in the many successful careers that launched there. Both chefs and front-of-house staff from Le Gavroche went on to excel in the industry, illustrating the restaurant's profound impact on the hospitality industry.

These individuals have carried forward the principles of dedication to excellence.

Front of House: David Ridgeway, Diego Masciaga, Jean Claude Breton, Remy Lyse, Michel Lang, Vincent Rouard, Ely Elimane, Thierry Georgeau, Emmanuel Perignon, Fred Sirieix, Peter Davis, Michael Newton Young, Thierry Tomasin, Emmanuel Landre, Francois Bertrand, David Galetti, Gareth Donovan, and Ursula and Silvia Perberschlager.

Chefs: Denis Lobry, Jean Louis Paul, Pierre Koffmann, Marc Beaujeu, Jean Louis Taillebaud, Marco Pierre White, Rene Bajard, Rowley Leigh, Christian Delteil, Steven Doherty, Gordon Ramsay, Marcus Wareing, Marc Prescot, Brian Maule, Bryn William, Nicolas Laridan, Monica Galetti, Rachel Humphrey.

The Roux brothers were very hands-on when it came to helping people succeed in the industry and, along with their own investor and later chairman of the Roux Restaurants Group, Michael von Clemm, often put their money where their convictions lay. In the mid-'70s, when Pierre Koffman left The Waterside Inn (having moved there from Le Gavroche) to set up his new venture La Tante Claire it was with a not inconsiderable financial investment from Roux Restaurants. As time went on they invested and supported many young one-time employees in their own premises: for Jean Louis Taillebaud, L'Interlude de Tabaillaud near the Opera House in Covent Garden London; for Rene Bajard, Le Mazarin in Pimlico; for Peter Chandler, Paris House inside the ground of Woburn Abbey; for Christian Germain, Le Chateau de Montreuil in Montreuil near Le Touquet in Northern France.

In this way, Michel, Albert and von Clem can be said to have not only been key in the careers of many world-class chefs but also to have helped start the UK restaurant revolution that began in the 1980s.

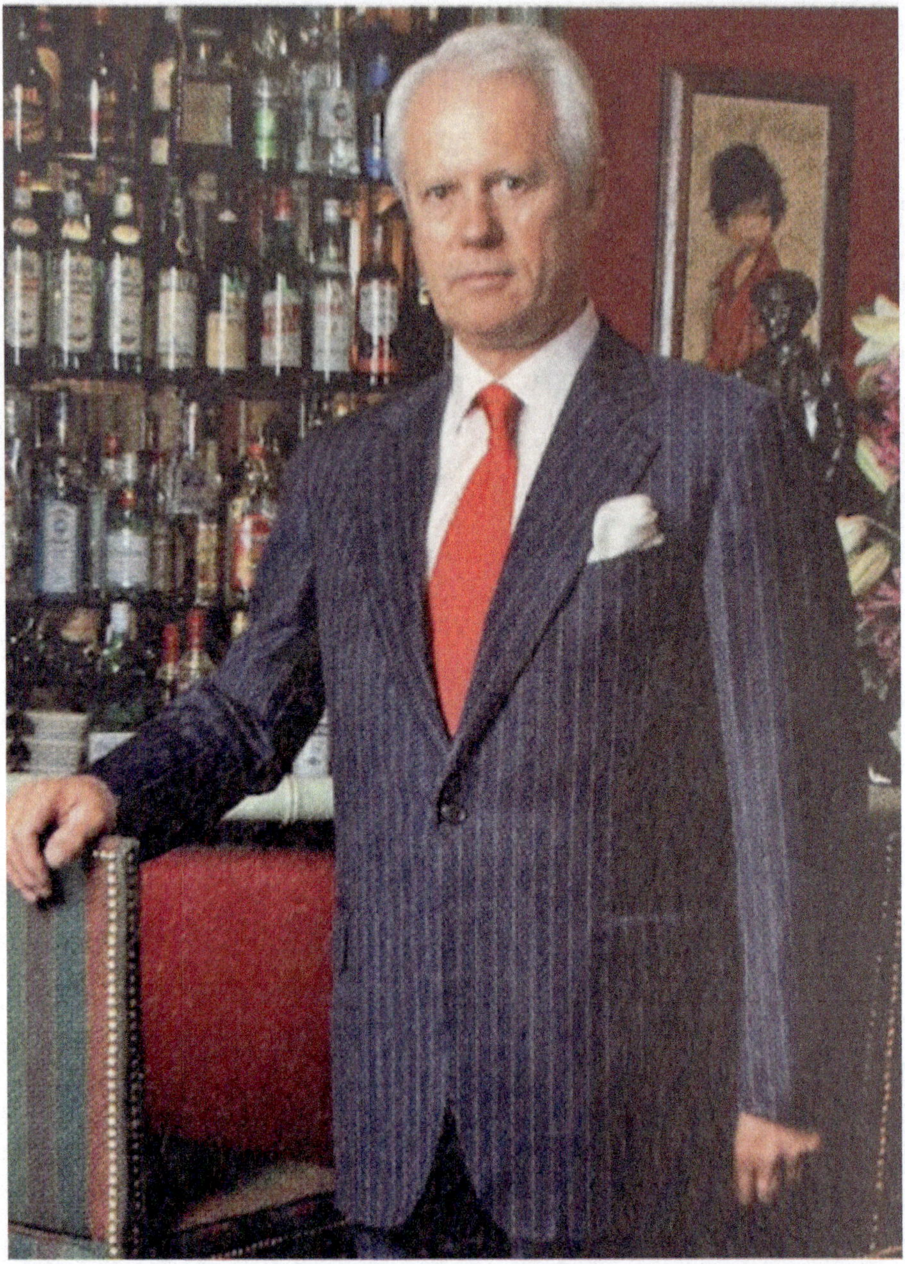

ABOUT THE AUTHOR

As a trustee of the Gold Service Scholarship, which awards up-and-coming front-of-house talent in the hospitality industry, Silvano Giraldin continues to inspire the next generation with his unwavering commitment to excellence. His dedication also extends to the Royal Academy of Culinary Arts, where he mentors future stars with the same passion and care that marked his illustrious career. Now retired from consulting but still ever-present at prestigious events, Silvano remains a beloved figure in fine dining—a mentor and a culinary icon whose family, friends, and love for exceptional cuisine ground him.

Printed in Great Britain
by Amazon